W

WONDERS
OF THE **WORLD**

Niagara Falls

Other books in the Wonders of the World series include:

Gems
Geysers
The Grand Canyon
Icebergs
Mummies
Quicksand

WONDERS OF THE WORLD

Niagara Falls

Wendy Tokunaga

**KIDHAVEN
PRESS**™

THOMSON

™

GALE

San Diego • Detroit • New York • San Francisco • Cleveland
New Haven, Conn. • Waterville, Maine • London • Munich

© 2004 by KidHaven Press. KidHaven Press is an imprint of The Gale Group, Inc., a division of Thomson Learning, Inc.

KidHaven™ and Thomson Learning™ are trademarks used herein under license.

For more information, contact
KidHaven Press
27500 Drake Rd.
Farmington Hills, MI 48331-3535
Or you can visit our Internet site at http://www.gale.com

LIBRARY OF CONGRESS CATALOGING-IN-PUBLICATION DATA

Tokunaga, Wendy.
   Niagara Falls / by Wendy Tokunaga.
      v. cm. — (Wonders of the world)
Includes bibliographical references and index.
Contents: The formation of the falls — Bringing Niagara Falls to the world — Harnessing the power of Niagara Falls — Determined daredevils.
     ISBN 0-7377-2056-5 (alk. paper)
  1. Niagara Falls (N.Y. and Ont.)—Juvenile literature. [1. Niagara Falls (N.Y. and Ont.)] I. Title. II. Wonders of the world (Kidhaven Press).
   F127.N8T66 2004
   551.48'4'0971339—dc21

                                         2003008453

Printed in the United States of America

CONTENTS

The Formation of the Falls

Thunderous waterfalls, swirling whirlpools, a gigantic cliff, and a mighty river all make up the amazing spectacle of nature known as Niagara Falls. Throughout history, this natural wonder has attracted princes and poets, adventurers and artists, daredevils, honeymooners, and tourists. Today, people continue to travel from all over the world to view its beauty.

Falls Facts

Niagara Falls is located on the border between the United States and Canada, between the cities of Niagara Falls, New York, and Niagara Falls, Ontario. The water in Niagara Falls comes from water flowing out of four of the Great Lakes—Superior, Huron, Michigan, and Erie. The falls are located along the thirty-four-mile-long Niagara River, which connects Lake Erie to Lake Ontario. About

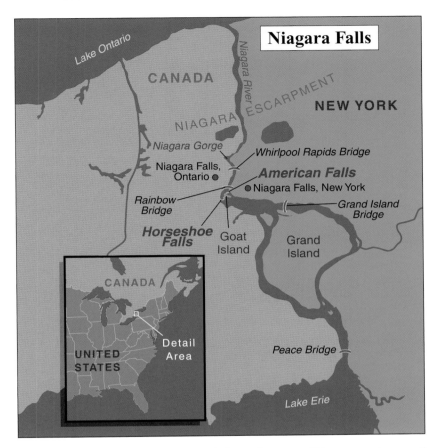

halfway along the course of the Niagara River, a piece of land called Goat Island divides the river in two. The divided river pours over a steep cliff and forms the two waterfalls that make up the mighty Niagara Falls.

The waterfall located on the American side is called American Falls. It is approximately 184 feet high—about 30 feet higher than the Statue of Liberty. Its crest line—the edge over which the water falls—is about 1,060 feet across. On the Canadian side is Horseshoe Falls. This waterfall is approximately 176 feet high, with a crest line of about 2,200 feet across. There are waterfalls taller than those at Niagara, but it is their

A group of tourists takes in the beauty of Horseshoe Falls,
one of the two waterfalls of Niagara Falls.

broad width and huge amount of tumbling water that make Niagara Falls so awesome. The combined amount of water in these two waterfalls is about six hundred thousand gallons of water per second.

After pouring over the falls, the water continues down the Niagara River and twists and turns into the Niagara Gorge. Trillions of gallons of raging water flowing for thousands of years have carved through the solid rock and made a deep and narrow path. The roaring waters in the **river gorge** make up some of the wildest whitewater whirlpools and rapids in the world. These churning waters rush in a counterclockwise circle, and some parts are up to two hundred feet deep.

The water finally makes its way into Lake Ontario, the last of the Great Lakes. Then it flows into the St. Lawrence River, some three hundred miles away. Continuing in a northeast direction, the water eventually travels another one thousand miles and empties into the North Atlantic Ocean.

Geologists—scientists who study the physical history, composition, and changes of the earth—say that the waterfalls at Niagara are about twelve thousand years old. However, the early beginnings of Niagara Falls can be traced back hundreds of millions of years.

Layers upon Layers

Five hundred million years ago, the Niagara Region— the area where the falls are located—and the eastern part of the United States looked very different than they do now. The Niagara Region lay under shallow warm seas. A massive mountain range called the Taconic

Mountains covered the eastern part of North America. Over millions of years, wind and water **eroded**, or wore away, the Taconic Mountains, reducing them into the Allegheny, Appalachian, and Catskill mountain ranges of today.

Water from rain and melting snow flowed down the western side of the Taconic Mountains. This water brought sediment—mineral particles and soil—with it. The sediment settled at the bottom of the warm seas in the Niagara Region. Over thousands of years, the sediment turned into layers of rock. Many types of rocks formed these layers. The lowest layers were made up of a soft type of rock called shale and harder rock known as limestone. Upper layers were made up of a type of limestone called dolomite.

Over time, wind and water sculpted the rock layers into the huge horseshoe-shaped rock cliff called the Niagara **escarpment**. Today, the Niagara escarpment stretches for some six hundred miles from Rochester, New York, into Canada.

Cooling Down

Throughout history, the earth's temperatures have usually been warm. However, there have been several cold spells. These are called ice ages and they caused many parts of the earth to freeze.

Almost 2 million years ago, the Niagara area experienced an ice age. At this time, huge piles of packed snow and ice—some as high as thirteen thousand feet—covered many parts of North America. Over time, these snow piles turned into solid ice called glaciers. Due to the pull of gravity, these glaciers began to spread out and slide over the land. The movement of the glaciers carved out huge holes in the earth underneath them.

When the ice age ended, the glaciers began to melt. Water from the melted glaciers filled the holes in the earth. This created thousands of freshwater lakes, including the Great Lakes. One of the Great Lakes—Lake Erie—overflowed, and the rushing waters formed the Niagara River.

The waters of the Niagara River were very powerful. Over thousands of years, the force of the river water battered the cliff underneath it until huge chunks of it dropped off. The roaring waters rushed over the cliff and became Niagara Falls.

A rainbow spans the Niagara River. The Niagara River was formed by melting glaciers at the end of the last ice age.

Is Niagara Falls Moving?

Niagara Falls is still changing today. As with all waterfalls, the running waters of Niagara erode the land underneath it. Scientists say that Niagara Falls has moved about seven miles southward since it was formed. This adds up to about three feet each year. However, iron rods have been placed underneath the falls to help strengthen the land. Controlling the amount of water that flows over the falls has also helped reduce erosion.

Today, the land underneath Horseshoe Falls erodes at a rate of only about one foot per year or less. The land underneath American Falls currently erodes about three to four inches every ten years.

However, the wearing away of the land is likely to continue. And due to the unpredictable forces of nature,

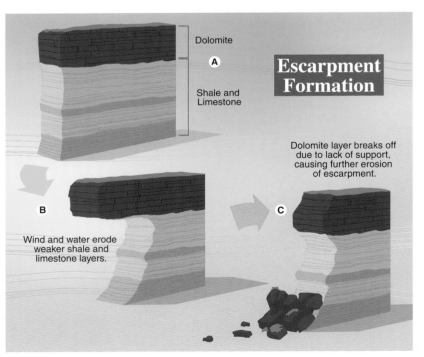

Dolomite

A

Shale and
Limestone

**Escarpment
Formation**

Dolomite layer breaks off
due to lack of support,
causing further erosion
of escarpment.

B

C

Wind and water erode
weaker shale and
limestone layers.

Each year, the running waters of the falls erode some of the land beneath Niagara Falls.

the true erosion rate can never be completely accurate. The water of the falls fills tiny, honeycomb-shaped cracks in the rock underneath. As the water filters through, these cracks become larger. The softer rock layer underneath the falls weakens and eventually breaks off, causing a rockfall.

Over time, the continuing falling of the rocks could cause Niagara Falls to move all the way back to Lake Erie and completely disappear into its own river of strong rapids. Scientists disagree as to how long this could take, but some say it could happen by the year 4500. Others predict this will take up to twenty-five thousand years to occur. However, for the foreseeable future, the mighty power and beauty of Niagara Falls will continue to be a wonder of nature, and will continue to thrill all those who visit.

Bringing Niagara Falls to the World

Some fifty years after the first Europeans landed in North America, explorers ventured into the continent's Great Lakes and Niagara Regions. They were excited by stories they had heard from Native Americans about a gigantic waterfall hidden in the woods.

An Incredible Waterfall

Father Louis Hennepin was the first person to write an **eyewitness** description of the falls in a book about his travels. Father Hennepin was a priest from the Netherlands. In 1678, he traveled to North America with French-explorer René-Robert Cavelier La Salle. La Salle set up camp and stayed behind at Lake Ontario, but Father Hennepin and a crew went ahead to explore the Niagara River.

When the men arrived near the mouth of the river, they heard a tremendous roar. Father Hennepin was both terrified and amazed by what he saw next. He later wrote,

> Betwixt the Lake Ontario and Erie, there is a vast and prodigious cadence of water which falls down after a surprising and astonishing manner, insomuch that the universe does not afford its parallel. . . . This wonderful downfall is made of two great cross-streams of water, and two falls, with an island sloping along the

Father Louis Hennepin and his men discover Niagara Falls. Hennepin wrote detailed descriptions of the magnificence of the falls.

This painting depicts Niagara Falls as it appeared in the early nineteenth century.

middle of it. The waters that fall from this vast height do foam and boil in the most hideous manner imaginable, making an outrageous noise more terrible than that of thunder . . . .[1]

A Long Journey

For more than one hundred years, Father Hennepin's tales provided the only firsthand accounts of the drama of Niagara Falls. Though Hennepin's descriptions fascinated people, there was no easy route to the falls. So, few people attempted the trip.

By the 1830s, however, tourists could reach the falls by boat and carriage. First they caught a boat that took them down the Erie Canal. After leaving the boat, they had to climb into small, cramped, horse-drawn carriages. It then took seven and a half hours to travel the twenty-one miles to reach Niagara Falls. By the time the visitors arrived, their faces and hair were covered with dust, and their clothes were caked with grime from traveling for so long on the bumpy dirt roads.

Crossing the Falls

Travel to the falls improved even more with the coming of the railroad. By the 1840s, the Great Western Railroad line on the Canadian side and the Rochester and Niagara Railroad line on the American side brought tourists directly to the falls. Tourists on one side could not cross to the other side, however. A suspension bridge was suggested as a way of connecting the two railroad lines and allowing people to cross the Niagara River.

Bridge builder Charles Ellet was hired to construct the bridge. He had built the first suspension bridge in North America over the Schuylkill River in Philadelphia. Ellet felt he could build a bridge that was strong and safe enough to carry trains from one side of the falls to the other. The bridge would have enough room for two carriage roadways on either side, two footpaths, and one railway track in the middle.

Charles Ellet was hired to build the first bridge across the raging waters of Niagara River.

Saved by a Kite

Ellet decided to build the bridge at the narrowest point of the Niagara River gorge near the falls. However, this spot was about eight hundred feet across. This great width created a serious problem. How would he get a cable across the river and up the cliff to the other side to start the building of the bridge? There was no way to throw a cable across the river. And the river's raging waters were too dangerous to be crossed by boat.

Ellet then came up with the idea of using a kite to carry the rope across. He decided to have a kite-flying contest. He offered a five-dollar prize to the person who could fly a kite across the swirling Niagara River gorge

People compete in a contest to fly a kite across Niagara River Gorge.

Two men sit on the cliffs as a steam train crosses the
railway suspension bridge over the Niagara River.

from the Canadian side to the American side. Dozens of people showed up to try their luck.

The contest lasted two days. On the first day, the winds were blowing the wrong way. But the next day the winds were just right. A fifteen-year-old American boy named Homan Walsh won the contest when he managed to snag his kite in a tree on the cliffs of the American side. Attached to the kite's string was a lightweight rope. Workers on the Canadian side then tied a stronger cord to the rope, while workers on the American side pulled the rope across the river. Soon after they were able to attach a wire cable and pull that across the gorge. This cable became the beginning of the bridge.

Completing the Bridge

The bridge was completed on July 26, 1848. The span was approximately 762 feet long, and rose 220 feet above the Niagara River's whirlpool rapids. Visitors were charged a fee of twenty-five cents to cross the bridge. In the end, however, the bridge was too light to support a railroad track. It was only used for horse-drawn carriages and foot travel.

Bridge designer John A. Roebling was hired to build a stronger, double-deck bridge that could safely support a railroad. The building of the railway suspension bridge began in September of 1852. On March 8, 1855, the first train crossed the bridge. The train weighed twenty-three tons—one of the largest of its time.

Roebling's bridge was the first railway suspension bridge in the world. It became a great tourist attraction itself. For the next twenty-five years, fifty trains a week crossed the bridge, bringing more and more people to the falls.

A Never-Ending Flow of Visitors

By the time Roebling's bridge was built, Niagara Falls was one of the most famous places in the world.

Now, in the twenty-first century, people from all over the world explore the wonder of the falls. They come by planes, cars, buses, and trains. The area around the falls is only about twenty-five square miles. But each year in the summer months, up to 12 million tourists come to take in its splendor. Visiting Niagara Falls is more popular than ever.

Harnessing the Power of Niagara Falls

The beauty of nature and the power of the rushing waters are why many people come to the falls. But Niagara Falls is more than just one of the great natural wonders of the world and a famous place to visit. Its waters produce millions of **kilowatts** of electricity that light millions of homes and businesses in North America.

Power in the Early Days

Early settlers who lived near Niagara Falls knew that the mighty waters were more than just mysterious and beautiful. They realized that the power of the falls could be harnessed and put to use.

French settler Daniel Joncaire was one of the first people to use waterwheels to harness the power of the water of Niagara Falls. Waterwheels use the power of

A dam in the Niagara Falls mill district harnesses the power of the falls to run the sawmills.

water rushing downstream in a river or waterfall to turn machinery.

In the mid-1700s, Joncaire built a sawmill above the falls on the American side. He used waterwheels to power the mill in order to carve lumber out of logs. Other settlers used waterwheels to power gristmills for grinding grain into flour.

Eventually more and more people built mills and factories along the shoreline to use the power of the Niagara River.

Hydroelectricity from Niagara

Powering mills and factories was just the beginning of putting Niagara's roaring waters to use. But there were still more reasons to tap the energy from Niagara Falls.

Inventor and scientist Nikola Tesla was a young boy in Croatia in the 1860s when he first saw a picture of Niagara Falls. He was fascinated by the sheer power of the water. Tesla told his family that someday he would go to the United States to capture the energy of the falls. Some thirty years later, he did just that.

Tesla believed that the tumbling waters of Niagara Falls could provide energy to power electric **generators** that could transmit electricity across long distances. He

Inventor and scientist Nikola Tesla experiments with electricity. Tesla believed the power of the falls could be used to generate electricity.

felt that this energy—called **hydroelectricity**—promised a bright future.

Tesla claimed that the water in Niagara Falls had enough power to "light every lamp, drive every railroad, propel every ship, heat every store, and produce every article manufactured by machinery in the United States."[2]

This was an exaggeration, but the Niagara Falls Power Company used Tesla's technology to harness Niagara's power. In 1892, the company began building the first two electric power generators at Niagara Falls. The goal was to bring hydroelectricity to Buffalo, New York.

Generators at the Ontario Power Generating Station use the power of rushing water to create hydroelectric power.

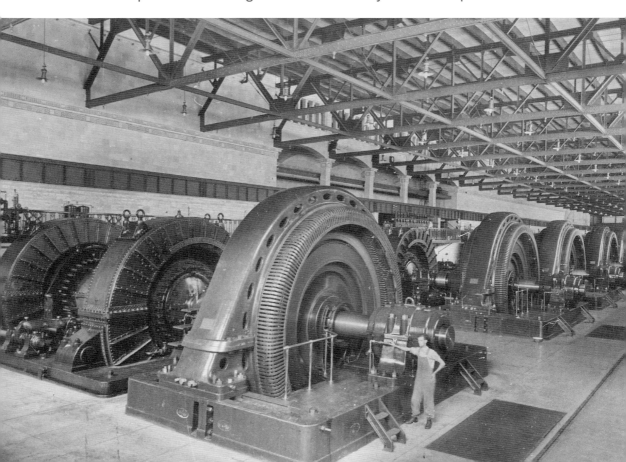

Although there were many doubters, Tesla was confident from the beginning that his system would work. "There is no obstacle in the way of the successful transmission of power from the big power house you have here," he told a reporter from the *Niagara Falls Gazette* in July 1896. "Power can be transmitted to Buffalo as soon as the Power Company is ready to do it."[3]

Still, there were those who thought the technology would fail. The power was ready to be turned on in November of 1896. But the mayor of Buffalo waited until shortly after midnight to flip the switch to avoid any embarrassment in case something went wrong. However, everything went as smoothly as Tesla had predicted. The streetcars and streetlights in Buffalo were now running on power generated by Niagara Falls. And this was just the beginning of the harnessing of the falls to provide hydroelectricity.

Hydroelectricity from Niagara Today

Today, energy from the rushing waters of Niagara Falls is turned into hydroelectric energy that is used by millions of people in North America. Hydroelectricity lights homes and businesses in many parts of the world. It does not cause pollution and is renewable. This means that the water providing the power is always available. Hydroelectricity is also fast and cheap to produce.

Huge hydroelectric power plants located in the area around Niagara Falls transform the water's power into millions of kilowatts of electricity. Just one kilowatt can operate three television sets, light ten 100-watt lightbulbs, or operate a hair dryer.

Niagara Hydroelectric Power Plants

The Niagara Power Project in New York state is a hydroelectric plant located four and a half miles downstream from Niagara Falls. When it first opened in 1961, it was the largest producer of hydroelectric power in the Western world. Now it is the biggest electricity producer in New York. It generates 2.4 million kilowatts of electricity—enough power to light 24 million 100-watt lightbulbs at the same time. The Niagara Power Project has two main parts: the Robert Moses Niagara Power Plant and the Lewiston Pump-Generating Plant.

Ontario Power Generation in Canada operates seven hydroelectric power plants that use the Niagara River for power. The largest are the Sir Adam Beck Generating

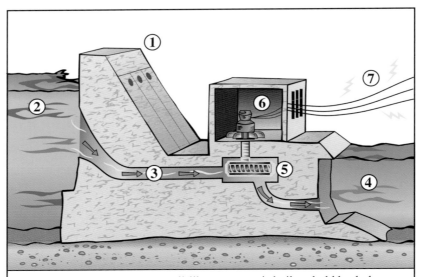

A dam (1), which is a large wall-like structure, is built to hold back the water in a river to form a lake (2). The water from the lake passes through tubes (3) in the dam and exits down the river from the dam (4). The movement through a tube turns a turbine blade (5). The turbine is attached to an electrical generator (6) that creates electricity when turned, and the electricity is sent out over power lines (7) to homes and businesses.

The Robert Moses Niagara Power Plant provides millions of kilowatts of power to New York.

Stations #1 and #2. They are located on the Canadian side of the falls. The various Canadian plants produce approximately 2 million kilowatts of electricity.

Together, New York's Robert Moses plant and Canada's two Sir Adam Beck plants are the largest producers of hydroelectric power in North America.

Preservation for Now and the Future

Harnessing the power of Niagara has been important to modern industrial progress in North America. But **preservation** of the natural beauty of the falls has been essential as well. By the late 1860s, both the American and Canadian sides of the Niagara River were packed with mills and factories that were built to take advantage of the power of the water. Goat Island—the piece of land that divides the two waterfalls—was also a popular place for building factories.

A small group of people were concerned that the natural beauty of Niagara Falls was becoming lost to ugly factories and buildings. They formed a "Free Niagara"

Picnickers enjoy their lunch on Goat Island. People have worked to preserve the natural beauty of Niagara Falls since the late nineteenth century.

organization that they hoped would be able to pressure the government to protect the falls' natural resources from **exploitation.**

Preserving the Beauty

The leader of the Free Niagara movement was Frederick Law Olmsted. He was best known as the designer of New York City's Central Park. Olmsted believed that the land around the falls should be a place of beauty where visitors could freely enjoy nature.

In 1883, after more than fifteen years of putting pressure on the government, Olmsted and his Free Niagara group won their battle. It was then that the New York state government bought the land surrounding the falls—including Goat Island—and tore down the factories and buildings. They created an area of natural beauty called the Niagara Reservation. This was the first time that a state government had bought land from property owners for the purpose of preservation of the natural environment.

In 1885, New York governor David B. Hill signed the Niagara Appropriations Bill. This made the Niagara Reservation area into the first American state park. This further guaranteed the protection of its natural environment. Since then, the governments of both Canada and the United States have worked together to preserve Niagara Falls as both a great source of power and a great source of natural beauty.

Determined Daredevils

As a force of nature, Niagara Falls is unpredictable and dangerous. For most people, just seeing the falls is thrilling enough. But a few have wanted to test themselves by challenging the power of Niagara Falls. Many of these daredevils risked their lives by performing crazy and unbelievable stunts on one of the greatest natural stages in the world.

The First Famous Jump

By the nineteenth century, Niagara Falls had become a major tourist spot. It did not take long for one group of businessmen to realize that the falls could earn them a *lot* of money. They decided to stage an event that would bring even more tourists to the area. They were counting on the tourists to spend money on the train, on food, on

This man poses for a photograph after riding a barrel over Niagara Falls.

lodging, and on souvenirs. They invited Sam Patch to be the first person to leap into Niagara Falls in 1829. Patch was a twenty-three-year-old mill worker who was famous for making high jumps into dangerous waters.

Patch happily accepted the invitation. He announced that he would jump 120 feet into the raging waters from a platform attached to the cliff of Goat Island, between the two waterfalls. In reality, the distance he would jump was more like 85 to 100 feet since the platform was actually located about one-third of the way down the cliff.

The huge crowd that came to see him in October of 1829 lined up on both sides of the Niagara River and on the banks of Goat Island. Patch climbed up a wobbly ladder to the platform. When he reached the top, he kissed an American flag, took a deep breath, and then stepped off the platform. Patch hit the water feet first at a speed of sixty miles an hour.

At first, the spectators wondered if Patch was lost or dead. But suddenly his head burst from the water and the crowd screamed and cheered.

Newspapers praised his amazing stunt. "Sam Patch has immortalized himself. He has done what mortal never did before,"[4] said the *Colonial Advocate*. "The greatest feat of the kind ever effected by man,"[5] claimed the Buffalo, New York, *Republican*.

Blondin the Tightrope Walker

Thirty years later, Jean Francois Gravelet performed an even more incredible stunt. Gravelet was a famous French tightrope walker. He was known to most people by his circus name of "Blondin." He first visited Niagara Falls in the summer of 1858. Niagara's roaring waters **mesmerized** Blondin, and he felt this was the perfect

French acrobat and tightrope-walker Blondin crosses the
Niagara River in 1859.

spot to perform a tightrope walk. He could not stop thinking about the falls after he returned to France.

Blondin returned to Niagara Falls in 1859 to walk from the American side to the Canadian side across a tightrope. Although paintings show him crossing the Niagara River right above the raging Horseshoe Falls, he actually performed his stunt a mile downstream from the waterfalls. Still, he was to cross without any safety net, and he would surely fall to his death if he tripped or lost his balance.

Blondin's tightrope was 1,100 feet long and 3 inches thick. Special wires attached to the shore kept it from swaying too much. The rope was strung 150 feet above the water, and it dipped in the middle.

A band played the French national anthem as Blondin stepped onto the tightrope. He carried a 35-foot pole to help him keep his balance. The people watching held their breath as he set out to cross the river. At the halfway point, he sat down on the tightrope. Then he lowered a rope to a boat some 125 feet below, pulled up a bottle of wine, and took a drink. He then got up and continued his walk as the crowd cheered him on. Blondin reached the Canadian side in about fifteen minutes. He then crossed the river again in a return trip that took only eight minutes.

Blondin Gets More Daring

Blondin continued his tightrope walking stunts for the rest of the summer. With each stunt he became more daring. On one occasion he carried a friend on his back as he crossed the river on his tightrope. Another time he balanced a chair on the rope and stood on top of it. Once he even cooked an omelet on a portable cooker and lowered it to a boat waiting below.

Blondin was one of many people drawn to the idea of testing themselves against the raging power of Niagara Falls.

Blondin crosses the river with a friend on his back. He became more daring with each crossing.

Annie Edson Taylor (shown here below Niagara Falls)
survived a terrifying plunge over the falls in a barrel.

Going over in a Barrel

In 1901, Annie Edson Taylor decided she would go over Niagara Falls in a barrel. Taylor was a sixty-three-year-old teacher from Michigan. She needed money and she hoped such a crazy stunt would make her rich and famous.

On October 24, 1901, with a big crowd watching, Taylor climbed into an oak barrel. It was fifty-four inches high and padded with cushions. She strapped herself into a special leather harness that would keep her from bouncing around inside.

Taylor's helpers launched the barrel from the American side of the falls, a mile and a half above the waterfall. As it moved downstream toward the waterfall, Taylor could hear the roaring waters. As the sound got louder she knew she was getting closer. She put a small pillow under her knees, held her arms to her waist, and placed her head on her chest.

The barrel flew over the falls. It seemed to hang in the air. Then it plunged into the water. When it eventually drifted to the Canadian side, rescuers pulled it to shore. They opened the lid and looked inside.

Confused, but Alive

Taylor was confused, but she was alive. She was so dazed that she could not remember anything about her ride. She was bleeding from a head wound, but had survived the stunt.

"If it was with my dying breath I would caution anyone against attempting the feat," she later said. "I will

The icy beauty of the falls in winter is a magnificent spectacle. Millions of visitors come each year to marvel at the splendor of Niagara Falls.

never go over the falls again. I would sooner walk up to the mouth of a cannon, knowing it was going to blow me to pieces than make another trip over the fall."[6]

Taylor became famous for a short time, but she never became rich. Instead, for several years afterward she remained in the town of Niagara Falls, New York, and charged tourists money to hear her story.

Daredevil Days Have Passed

Today, it is against the law to perform the spectacular stunts that Annie Taylor and others did long ago. The daredevils and their reckless adventures are part of the past. But it is still thrilling to simply witness the magnificence of the waterfalls. All who visit can marvel at the beauty, charm, and fury of the majestic sight of Niagara Falls—a true wonder of the world.

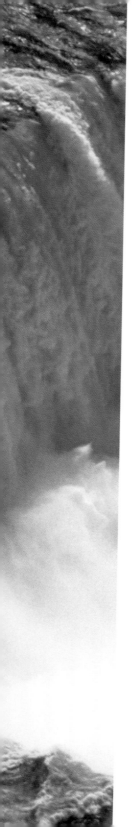

Notes

Chapter Two: Bringing Niagara Falls to the World
1. Quoted in United States Genealogy Network, "Great Epochs in American History: The Discovery of Niagara Falls." www.usgennet.org.

Chapter Three: Harnessing the Power of Niagara Falls
2. Quoted in Pierre Berton, *Niagara, A History of the Falls*. New York: Kodansha America, 1992.
3. Quoted in Daniel M. Dumych, "Waterpower at Niagara," Canadian Niagara Power Company. www. home.earthlink.net.

Chapter Four: Determined Daredevils
4. Quoted in Berton, *Niagara, A History of the Falls*.
5. Quoted in Berton, *Niagara, A History of the Falls*.
6. Quoted in Berton, *Niagara, A History of the Falls*.

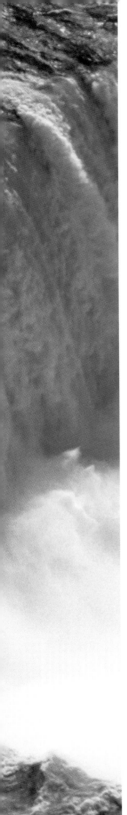

Glossary

erode: The wearing away of rock or soil by wind, water, or ice.

escarpment: A long, clifflike ridge of land or rock formed by the weakening of the earth's crust.

exploitation: Using something for the purpose of making money.

eyewitness: To view with one's own eyes.

generator: A machine that converts one form of energy into another.

hydroelectricity: Electric energy derived from the energy of falling water.

kilowatt: A unit of electrical power equal to one thousand watts.

mesmerized: To be fascinated.

preservation: To keep alive or in existence.

river gorge: A small canyon through which a river runs.

For Further Exploration

Books

Leonard Everett Fisher, *Niagara Falls: Nature's Wonder*. New York: Holiday House, 1996. Full of historical facts, drawings, and photographs about Niagara Falls.

Linda Granfield, *All About Niagara Falls*. Toronto: Kids Can Press, 1988. Includes "Twenty Great Things to Do at Niagara Falls," as well as an overview of the history of the falls.

Periodical

Jane R. McGoldrick, "Wild Water Niagara Falls Is Awesome!" *National Geographic World*, June 1996.

Websites

Niagara Falls Thunder Alley (www.niagarafrontier. com). Offers a detailed history, sightseeing information, and many photographs of Niagara Falls.

Nikola Tesla: Forgotten American Scientist (www. concentric.net). This site is maintained by third and fourth graders and their teacher at a Michigan school, and aims to preserve the memory of Tesla and his accomplishments.

Index

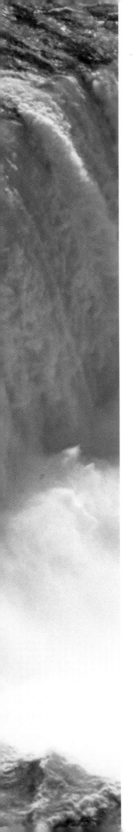

Picture Credits

Cover Photo: © Ron Watts/CORBIS
© CORBIS, 38
COREL Corporation, 8, 11, 13, 30, 40
Culver Pictures, Inc., 15, 18, 19
© Hulton/Archive by Getty Images, 20, 35, 37
Chris Jouan, 7, 12
Niagara Falls (Ontario) Public Library, 24, 26, 33
Suzanne Santillan, 28
© Scala/Art Resource, NY, 16
© Smithsonian Institution, 25
© Lee Snider/CORBIS, 29

About the Author

Wendy Tokunaga is a freelance writer and editor who lives in the San Francisco Bay Area with her husband. She has also worked as an executive producer for two children's websites. In her spare time, she writes fiction, studies foreign languages, and sings Japanese karaoke.